93

628

# "Over the Rhine

## THE LAST DAYS OF WAR IN EUROPE

Brian Jewell

**SPELLMOUNT**
Tunbridge Wells, Kent

**HIPPOCRENE BOOKS INC**
New York

**In the Spellmount Military list:–**

The Uniforms of the British Yeomanry Forces 1794 – 1914 Series:

The Sussex Yeomanry
The North Somerset Yeomanry
The Yorkshire Hussars
Westmorland and Cumberland Yeomanry
3rd County of London (Sharpshooters)
Duke of Lancasters Own Yeomanry
Yorkshire Dragoons

The Yeomanry Regiments – A Pictorial history

*First published in the UK in 1985 by*
*SPELLMOUNT LTD*
*12 Dene Way, Speldhurst*
*Tunbridge Wells, Kent TN3 ONX*
*ISBN 0-946771-70-7 (UK)*

*Published in the USA by*
*Hippocrene Books Inc*
*171 Madison Avenue*
*New York, NY 10016*
*ISBN 0-87052-128-4 (USA)*

British Library Cataloguing in Publication Data
Jewell, Brian, 1925 –
'Over the Rhine': the last of war in Europe
1. Great Britain. Army. 21st Army Group
— History    2. World war, 1939 – 1945 —
Campaigns — Germany
I. Title
940.54'21          D759.5 21st

All rights reserved. No part of this publication may be reproduced, stored in a retrieval system or transmitted in any form or by any means, electronic, mechanical, photocopying, recording or otherwise, without prior permission in writing from Spellmount Ltd, Publishers.

Editor: Kathleen Morley-Clarke
Production and Design: Sue Ryall

Printed and bound in Great Britain
by Anchor Brendon Ltd, Tiptree, Essex

# CONTENTS

**Field Marshal Montgomery's ORDER OF THE DAY,** *23 March 1945*      5

1   THE GRAND PLAN      *7*

2   'DUST MEANS DEATH'      *14*

3   '. . . O'ER THE WIDE AND WINDING RHINE. . .'      *19*

4   OPENING VARSITY      *27*

5   '. . . WINGS OF FLAME'      *36*

6   DIARY OF THE LAST 45 DAYS      *45*

**Acknowledgements**
The author and publishers wish to express their appreciation to the Imperial War Museum, London, for the supply of photographs, and to Tony Deane for maps.

# ORDER OF THE DAY

The following order was issued by the Headquarters of 21 Army Group on 23 March 1945:

1  On the 7th February I told you we were going into the ring for the final and last round; there would be no limit; we would continue fighting until our opponent was knocked out. The last round is going very well on both sides of the ring – and overhead.

2  In the West, the enemy has lost the Rhineland, and with it the flower of at least four armies – the Parachute Army, Fifth Panzer Army, Fifteenth Army, and Seventh Army; the First Army, farther to the South, is now being added to the list. In the Rhineland battles, the enemy has lost about 150,000 prisoners, and there are many more to come; his total casualties amount to about 250,000 since 8th February.

3  In the East, the enemy has lost all Pomerania east of the Oder, an area as large as the Rhineland, and three more German armies have been routed. The Russian armies are within about 35 miles of Berlin.

4  Overhead, the Allied Air Forces are pounding Germany day and night. It will be interesting to see how much longer the Germans can stand it.

5  The enemy has in fact been driven into a corner, and he cannot escape. Events are moving rapidly.
The complete and decisive defeat of the Germans is certain; there is no possibility of doubt on this matter.

6  21 ARMY WILL NOW CROSS THE RHINE
The enemy possibly thinks he is safe behind the great river obstacle. We all agree that it is a great obstacle; but we will show the enemy that he is far from safe behind it. This great Allied fighting machine, composed of integrated land and air forces, will deal with the problem in no uncertain manner.

7  And having crossed the Rhine, we will crack about in the plains of Northern Germany, chasing the enemy from pillar to post. The swifter and the more energetic our action, the sooner the war will be over, and that is what we all desire; to get on with the job and finish off the German war as soon as possible.

8  Over the Rhine, then, let us go. And good hunting to you all on the other side.

9  May 'The Lord mighty in battle' give us the victory in this our latest undertaking, as He has done in all our battles since we landed in Normandy on D-Day.

*Montgomery*

# 1  THE GRAND PLAN

In the spring of 1945 relations between the Allied commanders were at a low ebb. General of the Army Dwight D. Eisenhower, Supreme Commander Allied Expeditionary Force, was finding the Commander-in-Chief 21 Army Group, Field Marshal Montgomery, irritating: 'He got so damn personal to make sure the Americans, and me, in particular, had no credit, had nothing to do with the war, that I eventually just stopped communicating with him.' There were certainly clashes of personality throughout the Allied High Command, and the North West Europe Campaign was turning into something resembling a competition with commanders trying to score over each other. Eisenhower's unenviable task was to get the most out of the generals he had at his disposal.

Field Marshal Montgomery commanded 21 Army Group, comprising at this stage of the war the First Canadian Army (General H.D.G. Crerar) and the Second British Army (General Sir Miles Dempsey). Montgomery had been in command of all Allied land forces at the time of the Normandy landings but had, from the Autumn of 1944, lost to other commanders the American divisions, apart from some that were 'borrowed' from time to time as the tide of the campaign demanded. There were now four American Armies in the field compared with one each of British and Canadian.

For purely numerical reasons it was logical that the American troops should come under American command but, naturally, Montgomery resented what seemed to him to be a relegation to a lesser role. On the other side, American generals saw Montgomery as an arrogant and aloof commander who wanted to conduct the war in his own individual fashion, criticising all other ideas.

General of the Army Omar N. Bradley, who had commanded the American forces under Montgomery at the time of the Normandy landings, was promoted to command the newly formed 12 US Army Group, comprising the First US Army (which Bradley commanded in Normandy but now was under General Courtney H. Hodges), Third US Army (General George S. Patton), and Ninth US Army (Lieutenant-General William H. Simpson). There was another American Army in the field, the Seventh (Lieutenant-General Alexander M. Patch) but this was outside Bradley's command; together with the First French Army (General de Lattre de Tassigny), the Ninth formed the 6th US Army Group.

From October 1944 it had been Montgomery's delegated and agreed task to force the Rhine crossing but Hodges' First US Army had grasped a fortuitous opportunity and had jubilantly crossed the river over the Ludendorf Bridge at Remagen near Bonn on 7 March. Four American divisions, the 9th, 78th, 89th and 9th Armored, formed a bridgehead on the east bank at Remagen, much to the consternation of the Germans who then set about bombarding the Ludendorf Bridge from the air and by 17cm artillery, as well as attempting to demolish it by Kriegsmarine human torpedoes and frogmen. At last, on 17 March, the long-suffering Ludendorf Bridge collapsed, killing a large number of US Army engineers, but by this time a parallel military bridge had been thrown over the river. Thus the lines of communication for the four divisions were preserved but, in any case, they constituted a large enough force that was well able to look after itself and not be considered 'cut off'. On the negative side it did mean that the divisions' movements were restricted and they were 'lost' as far as being useful components for the back-up force for the main assault on the Rhine by the 21 Army Group.

Mention must also be made of the fact that General George S. Patton took the van of the Third US Army up to the Rhine at Oppenheim on the night of 22-23 March (the night before the main assault) and, under cover of darkness, slipped over the bridge there, where the river is about half the width it is at Wesel, the area where the main crossing was planned. As Patton was to claim, he 'made it before Monty got across'.

These excursions, particularly that of Patton, were what could be termed 'private enterprises' outside the grand plan.

In retrospect, it is easy to think of the Allied commanders, who did not like each other very much anyway, as being engaged in a race to overcome the Rhine obstacle. This may have been at least partly true as far as the American generals were concerned, but not of Montgomery who saw no reason to rush things. Undoubtedly, he could have forced a crossing a few days earlier than he did on 23-24 March but he was content to wait until all was entirely ready to embark on Operation PLUNDER, the code name for the actual crossing and the immediately following thrust into the heartland of Germany; a master plan carried through with very few variations.

Montgomery had under his command twenty-seven divisions: seventeen infantry, eight armoured and two airborne (thirteen American, twelve British and two Canadian, to put it in national terms). In addition, he had available five independent armoured brigades, a British Commando brigade and an independent Canadian infantry brigade.

For the assault the Second British Army was positioned north of Wesel, where the River Lippe joins the Rhine; on the left XXX Corps with its assault formation, the 51st (Highland) Division against the town of Rees on the east bank and, seven miles upstream, XII Corps, spearheaded by the 15th (Scottish) Division against Bislich opposite Xanten, while on the extreme right flank of the Second Army front the 1st Commando Brigade was to cross the river and attack the key town of Wesel.

A further seven miles to the south, the Ninth American Army, covering the right flank of 21 Army Group attack, had XVI US Corps with its 30th and 79th Divisions ready to cross the Rhine either side of the town of Rheinburg.

It will be seen from any general map of Europe that, if successful, the operation would open the gates for an advance through Munster and Osnabruck to Hamburg and Bremen, along the northern areas of the industrial Ruhr.

Two additional operations were formulated to support the main surface assault by the 15th (Scottish) and 51st (Highland) Divisions, the 1st

*Field-Marshal Montgomery with his Chief-of-Staff in 21 Army Group, Major-General Sir Francis de Guigand*

*Montgomery with his immediate commanders within 21 Army Group, Lieutenant-General Sir Miles C. Dempsey (British Second Army) and General H.D.G. Crerar (Canadian First Army) at the important planning meeting on 22 March 1945*

Commando Brigade and the American 30th and 79th Divisions:

1 At 1700 hours on D-Day Minus One (23 March) and again at 22.30 hours the Royal Air Force was to deliver heavy bombing raids on the town of Wesel to amplify the attack by 1st Commando Brigade.

2 At 1000 hours on D-Day (24 March) the XVIII US Airborne Corps, comprising the 6th British and 17th US Airborne Divisions were to fly in to dropping and landing zones in the Hamminkeln and Flurenerheide areas, their official brief being 'to disrupt the hostile defence of the Rhine in the Wesel sector by the seizure of key terrain in order to deepen the bridgehead to be seized in an assault river crossing by ground forces, and to facilitate the further offensive operations of the Second Army'.

Field Marshal Albert von Kesselring returned to Germany from Italy on 9 March 1945 to be made Commander-in-Chief West in place of Field Marshal Karl Gerd von Rundstedt, whom the Führer was making a scapegoat for defeats over the previous months.

Even in the light of enormous threats hanging over the Reich, Hitler was not altogether pessimistic about the situation on the Western Front. The Ardennes winter had shown that counter-attacks could still be launched, and there was always the natural obstacle of the Rhine! Of course, there was the little matter of the American bridgehead at Remagen that had been established a couple of days earlier but Hitler had little doubt this could be mopped up without too much trouble.

Kesselring's orders were to hold the Western Front with existing forces until the Eastern Front Armies were brought up to strength, after which

*Field-Marshal Montgomery, Commander-in-Chief 21 Army Group, with Lieutenant-General William H. Simpson, Commander of the US Ninth Army*

*Lieutenant-General Sir Miles C. Dempsey with Air Vice-Marshal H. Broadhurst at a historic meeting called by Montgomery on 22 March 1945 at the German village of Walbeck*

adequate reinforcements would be sent to enable him to launch a decisive counter-offensive.

On the night of 9-10 March, at his new headquarters at Ziegenberg, Kesselring was presented with a report of the position by his Chief-of-Staff, General Siegfried Westphal, a report that in no way substantiated the Führer's confidence. The new Commander-in-Chief learned that he had fifty-five divisions (at this stage of the war the strength of German army divisions had fallen to about 7,000 men) against a total of eighty-five Allied divisions. It meant an average of sixty-three men for each mile of front to be covered. To make matters worse, the Allies had undeniable superiority in the air.

Kesselring sought authority from OKW (Oberkommando der Wehrmacht – the High Command of the German Armed Forces) to withdraw the First and Seventh Armies to the east side of the Rhine to oppose the attack he knew would surely come, but Hitler was to deny this until it was too late. In the event, the only additional troops he was to receive were a single division softened by garrison service in Denmark.

Specifically, Kesselring placed responsibility for defending the Wesel sector of the Rhine in the hands of General Alfred Schlemm, a competent commander, who knew it would not be many days before the Allies made their assault across the river. The position was extremely disturbing.

The most dependable of Schlemm's troops, the First Parachute Army (this was an honorary title as very few men serving at that time had airborne training), was seriously depleted in men and stores, and his 86th Corps comprised a hotch-potch quality of troops. After much pressure, Schlemm was allocated the 57th Panzer Corps; this he placed in reserve

12

opposite the Canadians and the northern flank of the 51st (Highland) Division. Above Wesel, and facing Xanten on the other side of Rhine, he stationed mainly paratroops, while south of Wesel was held by infantry. By this time all bridges across the Rhine between Nijmegen and Cologne had been destroyed.

Two days before the assault by the 21st Army Group, General Schlemm's headquarters was hit by Allied fighter-bombers and the wounded Schlemm's place as commander of the First Parachute Army was taken by General Günther Blumentritt, who had been commander of the German 25th Army.

Every farmhouse, cottage and barn was made into a strongpoint. Schlemm was certain there would be an airborne assault and could predict where it would take place. What he could not know was when it would be launched. There was no time to erect anti-glider poles that were features of the Normandy landing zones – the gliders would have to be hit before they landed and that meant anti-aircraft guns. These he was not short of and emplacements were quickly established.

Field artillery was positioned on the relatively high ground of the Diersfordter Wald, a bank of wooded country through which ran the Wesel-Rees road. From here the batteries could cover the plain to the river bank and beyond.

# 2 'DUST MEANS DEATH'

It was on 13 March 1945 that two British infantry divisions took up station along the west bank of the Rhine: the 52nd (Lowland) Division, specially trained in Scotland for mountain warfare but whose first actions against the enemy had been on the flattest possible land in the Schelt Estuary, prior to the opening up of the port of Antwerp for Allied shipping, was occupying a front from Buderich to Vynen – about ten miles as the crow flies, but with two loops in the river and with the town of Xanten on the west bank and the even more important town of Wesel opposite, on the side of the river occupied by the enemy. The division was to be the eyes and ears of Lieutenant-General Sir Neil Ritchie's XII Corps while, extending to the north, the 3rd Infantry Division was given a similar role on behalf of XXX Corps commanded by Lieutenant-General Sir Brian Horrocks.

The work of the two divisions was wide and varied in the tense situation that prevailed throughout the ten days the 'watching' brief was followed. No one knew the real strength of the German forces on the other side of the river or what action they might take at any time.

The Rhine at Xanten is between 300 and 400 yards wide, with a current flowing about six feet per second; the floodbank to which the town of Xanten extends is some 300 yards from the river, and the total gap was sufficient cushion effectively to separate the opposing forces, causing each side to be unaware of the other's positions and activities. What surprisingly little air reconnaissance there was apparently did not disclose details of troop movements or their numbers. Nor was anything known about their morale.

Xanten's church tower was a valuable observation post with a panoramic view of the eastern side of the Rhine and the Westphalian plain beyond, but the glimpse of a truck or two, or the odd motorcyclist, was about all the intelligence that could be gathered from this vantage point. The German soldiers were obviously well dug in and hidden; the movements that had to take place were made at night or under cover of smoke.

The church tower at Xanten was not the most healthy place to be. Over the ten days leading up to D-Day the tower and its spire gradually gathered more and more holes from hits and near-missing shells. It seemed rather odd that the Germans did not put a more concentrated effort into taking out the Xanten tower, as the British artillery apparently had little difficulty in bringing down the church towers at Wesel and Bislich on the opposite bank.

The divisional artillery main brief was to make ready for the great bombardment that was to precede the crossing, preparing for themselves the most intricate of fire plans. This is not to say that the gunners missed any chance of firing at signs of movement on the other side. It was dry that spring and moving trucks threw up clouds of dust. All roads on the west side carried the ominous signs: 'DUST MEANS DEATH' – indeed, it sometimes did, as gunners on both sides were playing a similar deadly game. At other times, when the smokescreens were allowed to clear, the gunners would stage a dummy bombardment in an attempt to draw enemy retaliation so the gun positions could be pin-pointed, usualy without success, for both sides quickly learned the finer points of the new chess game. The smokescreen was intermittent during the early stages of the watch on the Rhine, and was continuous between dawn on 21 March and 1700 hours on 23 March.

For the Royal Engineers Field Companies of the 3rd and 52nd Divisions it was a hectic, tiring and, at times, dangerous period. Theirs was the responsibility to lay tracks to the river for the boats and amphibious vehicles which were to carry the assault troops; to tape routes beyond the floodbank which would be followed by the infantry, routes that were marked at intervals by small cycle-type battery lamps, masked and pointing away from the river so they could not be seen by the enemy. This work had to be done in silence under cover of darkness or smokescreen. The smoke was a mixed blessing, it gave a degree of protection but it was smelly and made the chest ache; it also attracted attention from the German gunners who became aware that something was going on which was not intended for the eyes of their observation posts. Sometimes machine guns opened up on fixed lines of fire or in haphazard sweeps, but bullets caused less concern than the 88mm airburst shells which Allied soldiers had learned to respect since the earliest days in Normandy and which were to dog forward-area troops until the end of hostilities.

The infantry of the watching divisions had several tasks, none particularly spectacular but nevertheless very necessary. One was to see that no enemy crossed over by boat or raft. This was German soil and, apart from the obvious possibility of reconnaissance parties slipping in from the east bank, it was important to see that no individual agents carried back vital intelligence in the other direction. An infantry battalion could have as many as fourteen section posts at the water's edge. At dusk the men made their silent way to the river to watch through the hours of darkness. It had to be done in complete silence without even the meagre luxury of a smoke.

Occasionally deserters would find their way across and, if they survived the first sighting by the sentries, they would be led back to battalion headquarters for interrogation about the disposition and strength of the German forces.

After accumulating such local knowledge and having the place to themselves, it was inevitable that the watchers on the Rhine should feel a little resentful of the newcomers, whose numbers were building up daily. Traffic was constantly increasing, and the huge piles of stores, parks of vehicles and the presence of Royal Navy personnel removed any doubt as to the imminent course of events. War plays tricks with time. To the watchers, the vigil on the Rhine seemed far longer than its actual span of ten days. It was obvious that D-Day could not be far away, the DUKWs, Buffalos and naval craft on trailers parked in numerous assembly areas and in the side streets of Xanten confirmed this fact, but few had an inkling when the moment would come.

The hardware needed for the crossing of the Rhine defies imagination. Some 1,300 guns of the British Second Army were to take part in the prelude to the assault, and a total of 60,000 tons of ammunition had to be transported and dumped in readiness for the gunners' use. To build the replacement bridges over the Rhine, 30,000 tons of equipment were needed. Altogether, military stores of all kinds totalled a quarter of a million tons.

A detachment of the Royal Navy arrived from Antwerp, after a devious voyage through a series of Belgian, Dutch and German canals. Vice-Admiral Sir Harold M. Burrough was in overall command of the forty-five LCMs (Landing Craft Mechanised), each capable of carrying a battletank but light enough to be transported by trailer over limited distances. The Royal Navy was also to crew some of the DUKWs (wheeled amphibious vehicles for cargo and personnel), and the tracked 12-ton amphibious vehicles known as 'Alligators' to the Americans and as 'Buffalos' to the British. Most of the latter carriers were supplied by the British 79th Armoured Division, commanded by Major-General Sir Percy Hobart, a formation affectionately known as 'The Zoo'. The Division carried stocks of a number of specially developed or adapted tracked vehicles – 'Hobart's Funnies' – available, as required, to formations of the 21 Army Group.

Other vehicles of the 79th Armoured Division used on Operation PLUNDER were:

DD (Duplex-Drive) Tanks, made amphibious by fitting a collapsible canvas screen round the hull, and equipped with propellers for propulsion through the water.

'Crabs' or Flail Tanks, adapted for minefield clearance. These were fitted with chain flails at the front which exploded anti-tank and anti-personnel mines.

'Crocodiles': flame-throwing tanks with fuel carried in a two-wheeled armoured trailer.

'Kangaroos': tanks with their gun turrets removed and used for conveying infantry.

AVREs (Armoured Vehicle Royal Engineers) which took a number of forms:
(1) Fitted with a mortar or 'petard' in place of a gun, for use against concrete pillboxes and anti-tank obstructions.
(2) Fitted with 'scissor-bridge' mounted on the hull which, when un-folded, could span a short gap.
(3) A fascine-carrier with a bundle of wood mounted at the front which could be released to fill a creater or ditch.
(4) 'Bobbin' tracklayer, with a roll of metal mesh carried for unrolling to form a trackway over marshy ground.

Life on the river-bank fell into a strange routine. Each morning the RE platoons would load themselves into their 3-ton trucks to be taken off to their work after breakfasting in an open field from 'Compo' field-pack tinned bacon and porridge. A sandwich lunch (usually cheese and jam, again from 'Compo' packs) was taken by each man in his mess-tins, to be eaten with grimy hands and washed down with tea from a hay-box 'dixie' that

16

*Winston Churchill talking to troops of the 15th (Scottish) Division at Xanten on D-Day Minus One (23 March), while Montgomery looks on from a jeep*

shared the back of the Karrier. The highlight of each day was the evening return drive along the dusty road back to the farm, where in the cookhouse field the cooks had ready the main meal of the day, when the 'Compo' ration cans were augmented to some extent by the cooks' foraging. The German civilians had been evacuated out of the operational area, leaving their livestock and poultry behind. Eggs, chickens and milk were in plentiful supply but fresh bread and vegetables did not reach small outposts such as this. Nor did newspapers, and after the meal the only thing to do was to retire to wherever one's bedroll was in barn or shed and chat on the subjects that are standard to all soldiers. Contrary to popular civilian belief, sex is not the predominant topic. More commonly heard are the memories of past peaceful times, hopes for the future, and criticisms of those in charge.

Sleep was never long in coming. Bodies were tired and aching after a day working beyond the floodbank and the short spring evenings ended as light began to fail at about 1900 hours.

Each morning, kit and bedrolls were made up and stacked, which seemed an unnecessary chore until the day when it was realised that, without warning, the platoon was not going to return to the temporary home, but it was to be three days before the kit, picked up by other company transport, was to catch up with its owners.

That was the 23 March, and throughout the day concentrations of men, equipment and vehicles built up behind the continuous smokescreen in an atmosphere resembling some vast bizarre fairground in fog. Behind the floodbank the smoke thinned to a mist with visibility of 200-300 yards. Units of company or platoon strength, depending on their role in the forthcoming

17

affray, were spread around in seemingly haphazard fashion but presumably predetermined by some plan mightier than the humble soldier could conceive. Field Ambulance Stations had their tents erected and were already tending unfortunates wounded by shrapnel from the German 88mm shells which opened up from time to time, or who had twisted ankles jumping from tanks, or had otherwise managed to damage themselves in some incongruous way. In such a large concentration of men preparing for battle there are always those in need of patching. Cooks went about their never-ending business of providing fuel for the troops: tea and still more tea.

Tankmen serviced their mechanical chargers, and infantry cleaned rifles and brens. The inevitable slit trenches were dug, more out of habit than necessity. Those with nothing left to prepare wrote letters or took short strolls – 'not too far' they were warned by sergeants and corporals, in case they were needed in a hurry.

Many can recall seeing Allied Supreme Commander Eisenhower in his distinct chocolate-brown combat dress visiting Montgomery's observation post a mile or so south of Xanten, from which, when there was no smokescreen, there was a panoramic view over the Westphalian plain.

At around 1730 hours, smoke dischargers were shut off; and at 1800 hours precisely, the entire artillery of the Second British Army and the Ninth US Army opened fire, their shells and 'magic carpets' of rockets passing over the heads of the assemblies of men. It was the greatest assault of shellfire since D-Day in Normandy. It was a breathtakingly fearful but, at the same time, exhilarating experience, affording a modicum of comfort in that it would surely soften the enemy's capability and will to fight in the forthcoming battle.

The colossal barrage of every calibre of shell was to be kept up until 0945 hours the next morning, with pauses only in sectors where the assaulting forces were sounding out the strength of the enemy defences.

# 3 '. . . O'ER THE WIDE AND WINDING RHINE'

The front on which Operation PLUNDER was launched extended some twenty-five miles, from Emmerich in the north to Rheinberg in the south. On 22 March, in the German village of Walbeck, Montgomery called an 'O Group' to give his final orders to his British and Canadian Army Commanders, Corps and Divisional Commanders and Chiefs-of-Staff.

H-Hour for the 51st (Highland) Division and a brigade of Canadian infantry on the British XXX Corps' front in the northern sector of the Second Army was at 2100 hours on D-Day Minus One (23 March).

Major-General Thomas Rennie was able to get four of his battalions across the river in seven minutes using 150 Buffalo tracked amphibious vehicles trundling down to the water and swimming their way across. Some made dry land without trouble but others became bogged down in the mud, forcing their passengers to wade the last few yards to the shore on foot.

Waiting to meet the Highlanders and Canadians were the 15th Panzer Grenadier Division together with the 6th and 7th Parachute Divisions, elite troops determined to sell the soil of their Fatherland very dearly.

It was a difficult and hard-fought battle around the riverside town of Rees and some of the Highlanders were cut off for a while by the paratroops at the village of Speldorp. In the course of the bitterly contested early hours of D-Day, Major-General Rennie was killed.

The German paratroops bravely defended their allotted positions, a battalion of them holding out at Rees until the morning of D-Day Plus Two (26 March) when troops from the Canadian 3rd Division cleared the village. It was to be a further four days before the Canadians were finally able to remove all the Germans from Emmerich.

This northern sector was to prove the most difficult and provide the most costly action of the entire surface operation on the night of 23-24 March; in fact, the Highlanders found that the Germans were fighting more fiercely than at any time since the campaign in Normandy. As XXX Corps commander, Lieutenant-General Sir Brian Horrocks was later to record: '. . . It says a lot for the morale of those German parachute and panzer troops that with chaos, disorganisation and disillusion all around them they should still be resisting so stubbornly.'

On the right of XII Corps sector the 1st Commando Brigade under the command of Brigadier Mills-Roberts crossed the Rhine at 2200 hours on D-Day Minus One (23 March). In contrast to that of the Highlanders to the north, the Commando's crossing went almost undetected and they were able to infiltrate the outskirts of Wesel, where the German 180th Division was ready to defend the town. Fifteen minutes later, 200 RAF Lancaster bombers flew in and 'neutralised' the town!

The unbelievable ferocity of the explosive eruptions and blast waves from the bombing of Wesel remained vivid memories for those who witnessed the

*Commandos manning Vickers machine guns amid the ruins of Wesel*

attack. War Correspondent Alan Moorehead watched the bombing from the second floor of a holiday villa on the west bank. In his book, *Eclipse*, Moorehead describes the attack: 'As we watched, the pathfinder came in, a single hurrying black moth in the air, and he shot his clusters of red flares into the centre of the town, which meant – and how acutely one felt it – that Wesel had just about ten minutes to live. The Lancasters filling the air with roaring and at last the catalysmic, unbelievable shock of the strike. Great black stretches of the skyline – buildings and trees and wide acres of parkland – simply detached themselves from the earth and mounted slowly upward in the formation of a fountain. As the rubble reached its zenith it suddenly filled with bursting light and a violent wind came tearing across the river. . .'

The Commandos were so close to the bombing that they narrowly escaped destruction themselves from the thousand tons of high explosive that were dropped but, attacking immediately, they were able to take possession of almost all of what was left while the surviving defenders were still dazed. Over the radio came the message from the Commandos: 'Noisy blighters, aren't they? We have taken the position and have met no trouble.'

The brigade established its command post only fifty yards from where the Germans had their headquarters. During the night the defenders of the HQ fought as hard as they could; even the commander Major-General Deutch, tried to shoot it out from behind trees in his garden, but was shot dead by a British Commando sergeant.

The elimination of Wesel was achieved with the 1st Commando Brigade suffering only thirty-six casualties, but the very efficiency of the annihilation was later to cause problems. Rubble resulting from the 'over bombing' made

*Men of 6th Commando in Wesel on the morning of 24 March 1945*

passage through the town impossible until US Engineer bulldozers had done their job and bridges had been thrown over some of the craters. Furthermore, the ruined buildings provided excellent hides for snipers – remnants of the 180th Division – making the town and the crossing of the Rhine at Wesel a dangerous undertaking for several days.

Around Xanten the 15th (Scottish) Division, under Major-General Colin Muir Barber, made ready to spearhead Lieutenant-General Sir Neil Ritchie's XII Corps on to the east bank.

The division's H-Hour was 0200 hours and already news of the adversities encountered by their compatriots in the 51st (Highland) Division to the north, and of the Commandos' success at Wesel, was filtering through to the men. It was therefore with mixed feelings that the Scots were shepherded into their craft by the Bank Control Group, which had been specifically organised to despatch troops and vehicles from the west bank at the various crossing points. It was an intensely dramatic moment for each man, as he boarded an allotted craft to set out over the mighty Rhine towards the unknown.

The LCMs and Buffalos were guided across the river by tracer bullets fired on fixed lines from the 'home' bank, and a lull in the bombardment revealed it to be a fine, still and moonlit night.

The first wave of Scots 'jumped out on the river meadow to the skirl of the pipes', as one eye-witness historian put it. Resistance was nothing like that being experienced by the other Scottish Division on the left, and fighting thrusts were made in the direction of the Diersfordter Wald, where German artillery batteries were hidden, waiting for the dawn light and the opportunity to discourage the build-up landings on the east bank, over which they

21

*A patrol of 6th Commando, 1st Commando Brigade, in ruined Wesel on the morning after the town was destroyed*

*Commandos clearing snipers from Wesel*

*A war correspondent discussing the ruined town with a captain of the Royal West Kent Regiment*

had a commanding view.

Not everyone who went over the Rhine in the first waves was an infantry-man. Beach Masters and their staff had to be conveyed; there were Artilliery Fire Control Officers, and the odd War Correspondent who needed a lift over so he could claim to his editor to have been in the van of the landings. Then there was the occasional Civil Affairs Officer with a case full of notices printed in German instructing the civilian population what to do under the Military Government of an occupying power. The Bank Control Group sorted out the 'odd bods', issuing priorities for places in the craft bound for the other side.

There were also reconnaissance sections of Engineers whose job it was to try to ensure there were mine-free tracks for the DD and craft-borne tanks, and to tape the safe routes. One such section, finding themselves isolated from compatriots, were exploring a narrow track from the river when a machine gun ahead suddenly opened up pinning the sappers in a ditch. Without the means of retaliation – they carried mine-detectors and a walkie-talkie instead of rifles – there was no alternative to sitting it out and waiting for some friendly support. It eventually came. 'What are you's doing down there you's dozey barsteds?' asked the infantry platoon sergeant in a strong Glasgow accent. Somewhat shamefacedly the sappers emerged from the ditch, only to return quickly to their hide as the sergeant fell beside them with a bullet in his thigh.

Anti-tank mines were what the sappers sought, but there were other nasty things to look out for: little wooden boxes, packed with explosives, that the mine-detectors could not pick up. These anti-personnel mines did not harm tanks and they often had little effect on wheeled vehicles, but they could,

23

*Defenders of Wesel in custody of the 1st Commando Brigade*

and did, blow a man's leg off. These weapons were first encountered in Holland a month or so earlier when it was realised that the only way of finding them was to probe with a bayonet, and there was not much time to do that on the east bank of the Rhine!

Soon prisoners were being taken as small groups of Germans surrendered to the invaders, turning from a trickle to a steady stream, to be conveyed back to the west bank together with the wounded.

Meanwhile on the same H-Hour 0200 hours D-Day (24 March) at Rheinberg to the south of Wesel, the 30th and 79th Divisions of XVI Corps, Ninth American Army, crossed the Rhine on both sides of the town, suffering thirty-one fatal casualties against minimal opposition.

The task of the 30th Division was to strike eastward on an axis parallel with the River Lippe, which joins the Rhine at Wesel, while the 70th Division headed for the small but important town of Dinslaken, three miles inland.

All American objectives were achieved without major problems and by dusk on D-Day (24 March) US Corps Engineers had bridged the Rhine with a 1,150-foot 'treadway'. Covering the US operations of 24 March and the building of the British Second Army's pontoon bridge at Wesel, the RAF Second Tactical Air Force and the US 29th Tactical Air Command flew almost 8,000 sorties at the cost of fifty-six aircraft. Altogether, twelve bridges were in service across the Rhine by the evening of 26 March, the bridges at Wesel being built at a remarkable speed despite the activities of snipers from among the ruins of the town.

Allied troops were not generally aware of Luftwaffe activity during the Rhine crossing but, in fact, fifty-two German aircraft were destroyed in the

*A Bren gun carrier ends its days on the east bank of the Rhine, inverted after running over a landmine*

*Scottish troops trying to spot an enemy sniper hidden in woodland*

air. Also, in two days, ten German airfields received no less than 2,700 tons of bombs, and a total of 168 enemy aircraft were destroyed by the RAF and US Army Air Force.

The dawn of D-Day (24 March) broke over the Rhine with battle engaged on a front twenty miles wide.

LCMs, and commandeered launches flying the white ensign, scuttled back and forth across the river giving the impression that the Royal Navy had been familiar with this stretch of water for a long time.

At a Field Hospital established behind the floodbank near Xanten, stretcher-bearers in khaki battledress and in Wehrmacht field-grey were bringing wounded into its tents, while both British and German doctors carried on their work of mercy.

Prisoners-of-war cages had been set up, their occupants looking shocked and numbed.

Winston Churchill had stayed the night of 23-24 March at Montgomery's Tactical Headquarters and was asked by the Commander of 21 Army Group when British troops had last fought on German soil. Without hesitation Churchill replied it was when the Rocket Brigade – in 1945 still in existence as 'O' Battery (Rocket Troop) Royal Horse Artillery and serving in Italy – fought in the Battle of Leipzig on 18 October 1813. The Rocket Brigade was the only British unit in that battle and was commanded by Second Captain Richard Bogne, who was killed during the action. The Rocket Brigade was attached to the Swedish Army and was fighting with the Prussians and their allies against the French, Saxons and Westphalians. There were thus Germans on both sides on that occasion. It was different in 1945 but rockets were still used in the bombardment before the crossing of the Rhine.

# 4  OPENING VARSITY

Prime Minister Winston Churchill with Field Marshal SirAlan Brooke (Chief of Imperial General Staff) and Field Marshal Montgomery (Commander of 21 Army Group) were at the 'grandstand' on the floodbank of the Rhine near Xanten when Churchill suddenly jumped up with boyish enthusiasm. 'They're coming, they're coming!' he shouted.

It was 1000 hours on D-Day of Operation PLUNDER (24 March 1945) and the Allied airborne attack over the Rhine, designated Operation VARSITY, had started on time. With triumphant majesty the paratroop-carrying aircraft, gliders and tugs of the XVIII Airborne Corps flew in from the south-west at 2,500 feet, but some at no more than 500 feet.

The Airborne Corps was to be put down around the Hamminkeln area, about seven miles from the east bank of the Rhine. This area, like most of the battlefield, was shrouded in the smoke of the action that had been raging through the night and in the suspended rubble dust resulting from the destruction of Wesel twelve hours earlier, obscuring the low ground, the most prominent feature of which was a wooded ridge, the Diersfordter Wald, rising some 60 feet above the level of the river. Along this ridge ran the road linking the towns.of Emmerich, Rees and Wesel. It overlooked the river crossing places being used by the British XII Corps and it was vital to relieve the Germans of this advantage as early as possible.

Another task for the airborne men was to take intact some of the bridges over the River Ijssel, which flows parallel to the Rhine between Wesel and Emmerich and lying to the east of the Diersfordter Wald. Between the river and the ridge lay level open farmland, providing ideal dropping and landing zones.

The final important objective was the small town of Hamminkeln, astride the River Ijssel. The plan for Operation VARSITY had been formulated in October 1944, when it was first realised that the crossing of the Rhine in the Wesel area was a strong probability. Exercises aimed at rehearsing the airborne forces were carried out in England between December 1944 and February 1945.

The British 6th Airborne Division's tasks were to take the northern part of the Diersfordter Wald, the town of Hamminkeln and one railway and two road bridges over the Ijssel. The US 17th Airborne Division was given similar responsibility to the south and were to link up with the British 1st Commando Brigade in Wesel.

Commanded by General Matthew B. Ridgway of the US Army and his British deputy, Major-General R.N. Gale, the XVIII Airborne Corps was made up of divisions that had recently seen action in Belgium and Luxembourg in support of the winter operations in the Ardennes: the British 6th Airborne Division, led by Major-General E. Bols, and the American 17th Airborne Division with Major-General William E. Miley

*US C-46 and C-47 towing aircraft and their gliders assembled on the runway of one of the specially built airfields in France prior to the airborne assault over the Rhine*

commanding. The Corps was carried by an armada of 1,572 transport aircraft and over 900 gliders, escorted by 889 fighters. Of the transports and glider tugs, 416 were British, from 38 and 46 Groups of the Royal Air Force: 38 Group, under the command of Air Vice-Marshal J.R. Scarlett-Streatfield, took the Air Landing Brigade of the 6th Airborne Division into action, while 46 Group, under Air Commodore L. Darvell carried the paratroops.

Unlike Operation MARKET GARDEN – the Arnhem area landings of the previous September – in this campaign there would be no risks, calculated or otherwise, to the success of the enterprise. It was a reversal of past strategy in which paratroops and glider-carried troops had been landed before or at the time of surface assault. In the case of Operation VARSITY, the drop came thirteen hours after the initial crossing of the Rhine by surface forces, and after bridgeheads had been firmly established.

Now, the airborne assault would be concentrated, with two divisions arriving within the shortest possible time margin, instead of in successive waves as in MARKET GARDEN, thus giving the German anti-aircraft defences little time to recover and prepare for the next onslaught.

Although the VARSITY plan seems a logical way of putting down an airborne invasion force, it did raise problems for the men taking part, particularly the glider pilots who, under the *coup-de-main* tactic, had to land their gliders very close to or directly on their targets. A new type of glider was developed for the operation: the Horsa Mk II which, like the Hamilcar, had a hinged nose, allowing vehicles and other stores to be unloaded immediately on landing. The Glider Pilot Regiment, which had suffered great losses at Arnhem in the previous September, was reinforced by RAF

*Horsa gliders, towed by RAF Halifaxes, passing over the French coast on the morning of 24 March 1945, en route to a rendezvous with the American airborne fleet over Belgium. In the background the Channel and cliffs of Dover can just be seen*

*Part of the airborne force on its way to the Rhine*

pilots who were given rushed courses on flying gliders and fighting as soldiers – the glider pilots' job was by no means over once they had their frail craft on the ground!

VARSITY was destined to be the last ever action by glider-carried troops as it had become obvious that the cost in lives and equipment was unavoidably and unjustifiably high.

The British 6th Airborne Division took off from eleven airfields in the south-east of England, where reveille had been sounded at 0245 hours, and the American 17th Airborne division from seventeen mostly specially-built fields around the Rheims and Amiens areas of France. Both components of the armada were in the air by 0800 hours, the British contingent rendez-vousing over Hawkinge in Kent, and the whole force meeting over Wavre (close to the site of the Battle of Waterloo) near Brussels, to make their combined way towards the Rhine. Thirty-five gliders failed to reach their destination through accidents. One Hamilcar disintegrated in the air over Belgium, all on board and the light Locust tank it carried being hurled to the ground; neither glider pilots nor their passengers had parachutes.

German anti-aircraft guns in the dropping and landing zones had been softened up by the previous air strikes and by the overnight artillery barrage. Now, fighter-bombers escorting the armada were given the task of spotting and attacking the many guns still active as the airborne troops were landing. Fire from the ground was indeed intense, forty-six transport aircraft being lost; of the 242 aircraft carrying the 6th Airborne paratroops alone, eighteen were shot down and 125 damaged by anti-aircraft fire. Of the 416 6th Airborne Hamilcar and Horsa gliders, only twenty-four were later salvaged in serviceable condition.

30

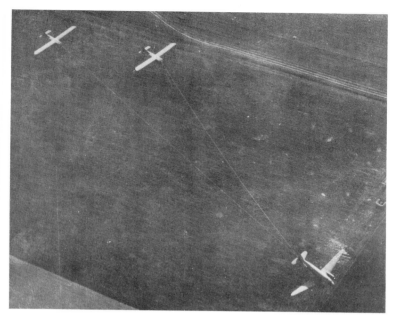

*A US C-47 transport towing two CG 4A gliders to a landing zone beyond the Rhine*

*The air armada bound for the Rhine. Dakotas of the British airborne fleet flying in formation after meeting the American fleet over Wavre in Belgium, while above can be seen Stirlings towing gliders and forming an aerial crossroads*

31

*The Rhine can just be defined through the haze in this picture taken by a Royal Air Force photographer from a glider tug at 1000 hours on 24 March 1945. This was one of the first pictures to be received in London of the assault over the Rhine*

*A sky full of aircraft as gliders loaded with US air-landing troops swoop down to their landing zone. Note the upward hinged nose of the glider in the centre, its load having been discharged*

*Hamminkeln soon after the start of the glider landings*

During the action, one C 47 transport, on fire and streaming flame and smoke, headed westward and rapidly lost height. Immediately over the floodbank the pilot managed to make his exit, his parachute opening just in time, and landed a few yards from a group of gunners resting after their long night's labour. The pilot turned out to be American and seemed less concerned by the narrow escape from death and the loss of the aircraft, which had by then crashed a few hundred yards away, than he was by the fact that he would miss a heavy date he had lined up in London that evening.

The gunners, who had long forgotten what a Saturday night on the town was like, were less than sympathetic!

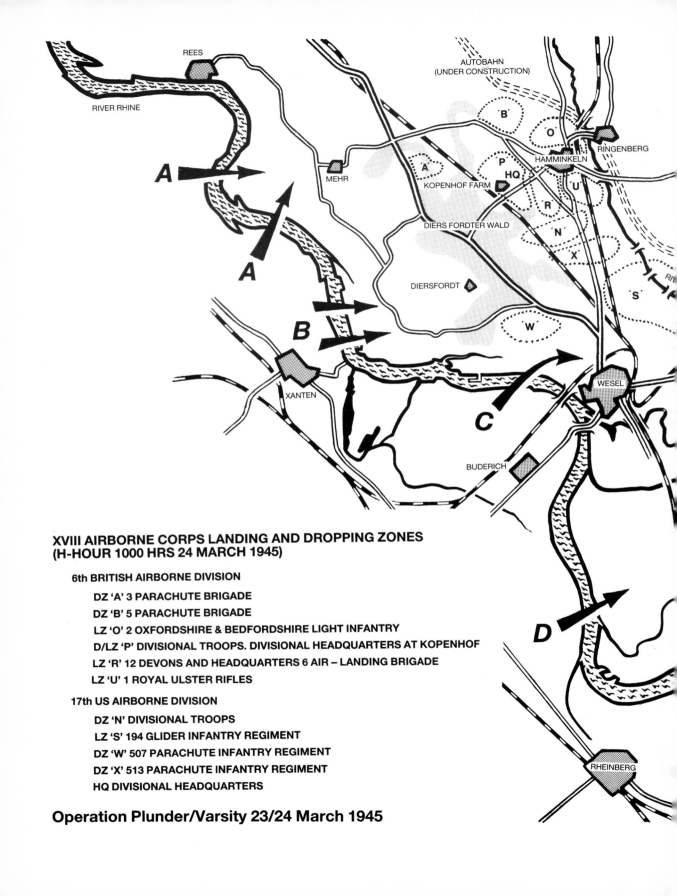

## XVIII AIRBORNE CORPS LANDING AND DROPPING ZONES (H-HOUR 1000 HRS 24 MARCH 1945)

**6th BRITISH AIRBORNE DIVISION**

    DZ 'A' 3 PARACHUTE BRIGADE

    DZ 'B' 5 PARACHUTE BRIGADE

    LZ 'O' 2 OXFORDSHIRE & BEDFORDSHIRE LIGHT INFANTRY

    D/LZ 'P' DIVISIONAL TROOPS. DIVISIONAL HEADQUARTERS AT KOPENHOF

    LZ 'R' 12 DEVONS AND HEADQUARTERS 6 AIR – LANDING BRIGADE

    LZ 'U' 1 ROYAL ULSTER RIFLES

**17th US AIRBORNE DIVISION**

    DZ 'N' DIVISIONAL TROOPS

    LZ 'S' 194 GLIDER INFANTRY REGIMENT

    DZ 'W' 507 PARACHUTE INFANTRY REGIMENT

    DZ 'X' 513 PARACHUTE INFANTRY REGIMENT

    HQ DIVISIONAL HEADQUARTERS

## Operation Plunder/Varsity 23/24 March 1945

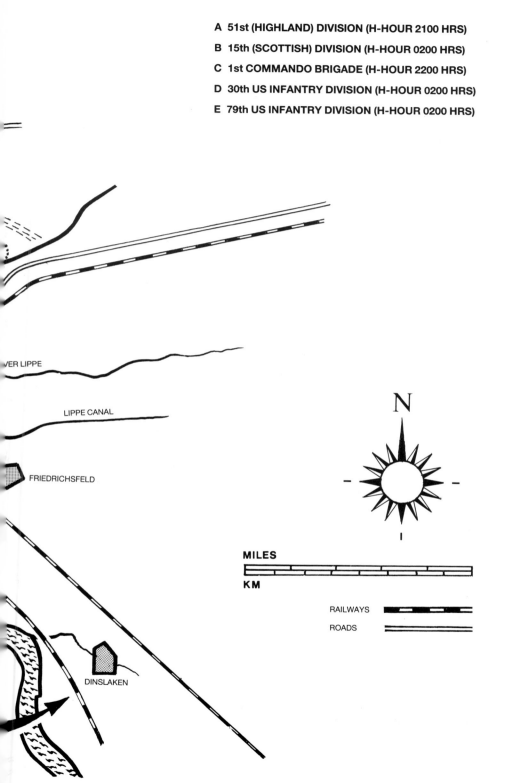

A  51st (HIGHLAND) DIVISION (H-HOUR 2100 HRS)

B  15th (SCOTTISH) DIVISION (H-HOUR 0200 HRS)

C  1st COMMANDO BRIGADE (H-HOUR 2200 HRS)

D  30th US INFANTRY DIVISION (H-HOUR 0200 HRS)

E  79th US INFANTRY DIVISION (H-HOUR 0200 HRS)

VER LIPPE

LIPPE CANAL

FRIEDRICHSFELD

DINSLAKEN

N

MILES

KM

RAILWAYS

ROADS

# 5 '. . .WINGS OF FLAME. . .'

Of the British 6th Airborne Division parachute brigades, the 3rd under Brigadier S.J.L. Hill and the 5th under Brigadier J.H.N. Poett, were to land first, to be closely followed by the gliders of the 6th Air Landing Brigade under Brigadier R.M. Bellamy. With the paratroops were officers of the Forward Observer Unit whose task it was to control, by radio, artillery fire from the surface forces. Airborne artillery and other divisional troops were to be landed in the centre of the area.

Some of the first paratroops to land were off their targets but in one case, at least, the error was providential. The 513th US Regiment dropped in the British 6th Airborne Division's area directly on batteries of 88mm guns which were wreaking havoc among the gliders. The Americans were able to silence the guns, thus saving many British lives.

The battlefield haze resulting from the nightlong shelling and dust that had drifted from the blasted town of Wesel, made matters difficult for the airborne men. Paratroops could not see the ground below them – they simply had to go down through the haze and hope they were not landing in trees or on German bayonets. For the pilots of the CG 4, Horsa and Hamilcar gliders there was great difficulty in finding their allotted Landing Zones and many crashed, cartwheeling as a wingtip touched the unseen ground, or shot out of the air by the German gunners. Matters were made worse by the smoke from many of the gliders themselves set ablaze by German incendiary bullets.

A description of the approach and glider landing was given by Brigadier G.K. Bourne in *By Air to Battle*, the official account of the British Airborne Divisions, published in 1945, shortly after the operation. 'I could see the Rhine, a silver streak, and beyond it a thick, black haze, for all the world like Manchester or Birmingham from the air [this was in the time before smoke-less zones were introduced in Britain]. For the moment, I wondered whether the bombing of Wesel, which had preceded the attack upon that town by Commando troops, had been mis-timed. . .In accordance with orders, but against my will, for I wanted to see what was happening, I had strapped myself in. We began to go down in a steep glide, and I listened with strained interest to the excited converse of our two pilots, neither of whom had been on operation before. . .Presently, I heard the first pilot say to the second "I can see the railway". Then I felt much relieved, and soon I saw the landscape flying past the windows. We landed very fast, went through a couple of fences and stopped with a jerk. All of us, consisting of the Defence Platoon of Divisional Headquarters, nipped out and took cover under a low bank on top of which was a post and rail fence. There was a lot of shooting about a mile away. We had arrived only about 600 yards from the pre-ordained spot.'

It is a tribute to the remarkable skill of the glider pilots that so many

*American paratroops after a concentrated drop*

landed accurately in the Landing Zones. The 6th Airborne Divisional commander, Major-General Eric Bols and his HQ party were piloted by county cricketer Major Hugh Bartlett, who brought the glider down very close to the projected command post at Köpenhof Farm.

The gliders carrying the *coup-de-main* parties, comprising the Royal Ulster Rifles and the Oxfordshire and Buckinghamshire Light Infantry, were also landed with a high degree of success.

It took two hours to land the XVIII Airborne Corps, the primary operation being closely followed by a huge supply drop by Liberator bombers. There was to be no repetition of the heart-rending misplaced drops that occurred at Arnhem.

The airborne men were in action at once, Hamminkeln being taken by the glider troops by midday. By 1345 hours the village of Schappenberg was in British hands and by the middle of the afternoon nearly all the main objectives had been achieved.

Strange things happen in the heat of battle. Alan Lloyd, in his book *The Gliders*, tells of one glider pilot's experience: 'Apprehensively, St John approached a farmhouse. He was confronted there by an imperturbable German matron, the first enemy he had met face to face. "She put a plate of steak and chips in front of me. . .I certainly hadn't expected a cooked meal. We were lads and she fussed like anybody's mum might".'

The Germans may not have been all that thick on the ground and there was a lack of armour to counter the airborne troops. What defenders there were, however, were some of the best the Wehrmacht had at this stage of the war: the 7th Parachute Division to the north of the area, and the 84th Infantry Division to the south, both reinforced with some hastily formed

37

*A photograph taken from beneath one of the crash-landed gliders. Air-landing troops are seen making their way to pre-arranged objectives*

*A ploughed field outside Hamminkeln, looking peaceful enough but, with tenacious German forces never far away, not the safest of places to be at noon on 24 March 1945*

*Medical orderlies of the British 6th Air-Landing Brigade leave their glider for what was surely to be a demanding day*

units. The German commander was well aware of the probability of an airborne assault and had small combat groups of his best-trained efficient soldiers posted at all places where a landing might reasonably be expected; their brief was to attack the invaders when they were most vulnerable – before they had time to muster themselves into a combatant force. They put up a formidable resistance in a countryside tailor-made for defence; fields and plantations criss-crossed by ditches and narrow roads. The 8th Battalion, of the Parachute Regiment, was heavily engaged in this terrain and was isolated until the following day. Not all the airborne men found their movements so restricted and there was a gradual infiltration of the Diersfordter Wald to meet the surface assault forces.

To sum up the position as night fell on Saturday 24 March: 21 Army Group had established a bridgehead of nearly thirty miles wide, the depth in the XII Corps sector being nearly eight miles. The Germans of the First Parachute Army were still resisting with the same vigour they had shown since the previous night but now, with the depth of the bridgehead advanced, the Allied Engineers were able to set about bridging the Rhine without hindrance from German artillery.

In the evening, Lieutenant-Colonel P. Luard, in command of the 13th Battalion of the 5th Parachute Brigade, found he had sufficient time to take a respite and prepared ham and eggs for himself and the Divisional Commander in the kitchen of Köpenhof Farm. At midnight, Major-General Ridgway was able to make a tour of the parachute and glider forces.

The XVIII Airborne Corps had brought in a number of glider-carried light tanks. In the case of the British 6th Airborne Division these tanks were operated by the Armoured Reconnaissance Regiment who proved their

*Gliders of the British 6th Air-Landing Brigade in a landing zone near Wesel*

worth when, with a company of the Devons and a group of Glider Pilots, four Locusts were able to contain some German tanks and a considerable force of infantry through the night until they could be mopped up the following day. Also during the night the Germans made a counter-attack on the River Ijssel with infantry supported by Tiger tanks. Although the attack was beaten off, a bridge west of Ringenberg had to be blown up to prevent its recapture which, to a minor degree, defeated an objective of the operation.

It was a night of mixed fortunes at individual level but the main plan was working well. In the night, most of the German 84th Division, with its gunners who had been causing delays to the surface assault, passed through the Airborne lines. Many Germans surrendered but, as neither side was in any state to make battle, large numbers plodded their way eastwards, weary and shattered by the experiences of the past two days.

By dawn on Palm Sunday, 25 March, news of increasing surrenders was giving buoyancy to the mood and morale of the men of the 6th Airborne Division, notwithstanding incidents when Germans crept out of hiding to infiltrate the Airborne lines, setting fire to wrecked gliders to show up their targets.

Now fresh waves of surface forces were passing through those who had initiated the assault. The Ist Battalion The Cheshire Regiment had crossed the river to support the Ist Commando Brigade in Wesel on the afternoon of the 24th, and 152nd Brigade of the 51st (Highland) Division was advancing north of the Diersfordter Wald. By 1000 hours advanced armour and infantry of the Second British Army and Ninth US Army reached the airborne forces, and by afternoon the links were strong. In the British sector it was the 6th Guards Armoured Brigade and men of the King's Own Scottish

*Gliders after the airborne landings in the area of Hamminkeln*

*Liberators of the supply drop fleet flying over a landing zone shortly after the airborne assault*

*Men of the 15th (Scottish) Division moving forward through wooded country after the night's engagement, having crossed the Rhine at 0200 hours*

*A long line of Germans taken by the British 6th Airborne Division, on their way to be conveyed across the Rhine to POW cages on the west bank*

*Lieutenant-General Miles C. Dempsey, commander of the British Second Army, crossing the Rhine by DUKW*

Borderers who came round the north side of the Diersfordter Wald and cleared the route for the evacuation of the tired men of the 6th Airborne Division. On the west bank they were to find camps with showers, kitchens and stores of fresh clothing. One of these camps was given the name 'Rhine Hotel' and displayed a sign proclaiming 'Glider Pilots a Speciality'.

Operation VARSITY had been completed but it was not the end of the road for the British 6th Airborne division which was reorganised to join the 2nd Army and ended the war meeting Russian troops at Wismar on the Baltic, 350 miles beyond the Rhine.

The war was not over with the crossing of the Rhine. There were to be more battles, some difficult and memorable for the participants, and there were times when some of the victors were to show signs of battle weariness for the first time in the face of remarkably brave resistance encountered along the way. The end seemed to be an intolerably long time in coming, with battles for each village and city suburb.

Even so, the die was irrevocably cast and it is appropriate to close this brief account of surmounting the last great obstacle in Europe with the words of Winston Churchill, left in Montgomery's autograph book at his Tactical Headquarters:

'The Rhine and all its fortress lines lie behind the 21st Group of Armies. Once again they have been the hinge on which massive gates revolved. Once again they have proved that physical barriers are vain without the means and spirit to hold them.

'A beaten army, not long ago master of Europe, retreats before its pursuers. The goal is not long to be denied to those who have come so far and fought so well under proud and faithful leaderships.

'FORWARD ON WINGS OF FLAME TO FINAL VICTORY.'

*This photograph, taken on 25 March (D Day Plus One) shows British sappers building 'Lambeth Bridge', a ponton or 'floating' Bailey bridge badly needed to consolidate the bridgehead on the east bank of the Rhine*

# 6 DIARY OF THE LAST 45 DAYS

Montgomery was later to sum up the Rhine crossing, probably his best organised achievement, in just sixteen words: 'Our attack across the Rhine, supported by a very large-scale airborne operation, was an outstanding success.' Modest words from a commander not naturally given to understatement. In the event, he had committed only four of the eight army corps available to him, but the organisation, forces, supplies and dangers involved were only slightly less than those on the Normandy beaches.

Winston Churchill had shown he was aware of the landmark significance of the crossing. Now he was anxious to set foot on the Wesel bridgehead but although he visited the east bank was turned back from the town itself by Lieutenant-General William H. Simpson, the US Area Commander, who refused to accept responsibility for the British Prime Minister's personal safety, as snipers were still active in the ruins of the town. However, within a fortnight, railway trains would be regularly crossing the river at Wesel over a new semi-permanent bridge replacing the one that had been blown up by the Germans before digging in to defend the great natural obstacle of the Rhine.

It now remains to outline the events between the Rhine crossing and VE Day on 8 May 1945; it can only be an outline as each day brought fresh action to each of the seven Allied Armies in the west and to the huge Soviet forces in the east, to the extent that it would be impossible to do justice to all victorious units and formations taking part in the tragedy or, for that matter, to pay due tribute to the brave tenacity, arguably misplaced, by the German defenders.

It is a complex web of action with great events being brought about simultaneously. Even on D-Day of the Rhine crossing, when the 21st Army Group's four bridgeheads over the Rhine were being formed into a thirty mile wide salient, General George S. Patton's Third US Army, well to the south, was capturing the town of Darmstadt, and the 8th United States Air Force B 24 bombers were wrecking underground oil storage tanks in Hamburg.

The following day the German Fifteenth Army at Remagen collapsed, allowing the First US Army of General Courtney H. Hodges the freedom to break out of their bridgehead.

On D-Day Plus Two, 26 March 1945, General Miles C. Dempsey, commander of the Second British Army, issued a statement through his chief intelligence officer: 'This is the collapse! The German line is broken. The enemy no longer has a coherent system of defence between the Rhine and the Elbe. It is difficult to see what there is to stop us now.' Confident words, but there was still some way to go.

This was an undeniably good day for the Allies. The Ninth US Army and Second British Army were progressing along both banks of the River Lippe in the process of overwhelming the German First Parachute Army; British

*Winston Churchill, Field-Marshal Montgomery and Field-Marshal Sir Alan Brooke lunching on the deceptively peaceful-looking west floodbank of the Rhine on D Day, 24 March 1945*

*British Prime Minister Winston Churchill on the demolished railway bridge at Wesel.
When this photograph was taken on 24 March 1945 the bridge was still under German
artillery fire and snipers were active in the ruins of the town*

troops had at last occupied Rees, which had been a thorn in the side for the
51st (Highland) Division at the time of the Rhine crossing. 21 Army Group
now had seven 40 ton capacity bridges over the Rhine, and last but not least
of the day's achievements was that of General Patch's Seventh US Army XV
Corps which crossed the Rhine at Gernsheim below Worms.

It was also the day when BBC Radio announced the death at 83 of Earl
Lloyd George of Dwyfer, who had been Britain's Prime Minister in the First
World War.

**Tuesday 27 March** The First and Third US Armies came close to linking up
near Koblenz; Wiesbaden fell to the Americans; the Russians launched their
final attacks on Danzig and Gdynia. In the air, RAF Lancasters dropped
'Grand Slam' bombs on U-Boat pens at Vegesack (Bremen) and attacked
Paderborn railway junction east of Hamm. In England, the last of the V2
rockets fell at Orpington, Kent, and on a block of flats at Stepney in East
London where 131 occupants were killed. The number of casualties from the
horrific V2 weapons reached a total of 2,754 dead and 6,523 badly injured. It
was also the day when the Argentine government decided to declare war on
Germany and Japan.

**Wednesday 28 March** The Guards Armoured Division, commanded by
Major-General Allan Adair, was now well on the road to Munster, and the
Second British Army as a whole began to drive towards the Elbe. The US
8th Armoured Division, commanded by Major-General J.M. Devine, had
reached the region of Haltern, twenty-five miles east of the Rhine. In the
east, Marshal Rokossovsky captured Gdynia and Marshal Malinovsky took
Gyor in Hungary. It was a day of changes, with the Western Allies switching

their goal from Berlin to Leipzig and, on the German side, General Hans Krebs replaced Colonel-General Heinz Guderian as Chief-of-Staff after a row with Hitler over defence policy.

**Thursday 29 March** Patton's Third US Army captured Frankfurt-on-Main and Patch's US Seventh Army occupied both Mannheim and Heidelberg. The Russians crossed the frontier into Austria. In London, the 2,419th and last V1 flying bomb (or 'doodlebug') fell; casualties from V1 bombs totalled 6,184 dead and 17,918 badly injured.

**Friday 30 March** General George Patton issued an Order of the Day claiming that in seven weeks the Third US Army had occupied 14,484 square kilometres of German soil, had taken 3,872 inhabited places, killed or wounded 99,000, taken 140,000 prisoners and eliminated two German Armies.

Danzig was captured by Marshal Rokossovsky's 2nd Byelorussian Front. The 8th USAAF bombed Wilhelmshaven, Hamburg and Bremen, sinking the cruiser *Köln*, fourteen U-Boats and eleven other vessels.

**Saturday 31 March** The First French Army, part of 6 Army Group, crossed the Rhine near Speyer with improvised boats and, by nightfall, had five battalions in the town of Baden Baden. The Russians captured Ratibor on the Upper Oder.

**Sunday 1 April** The US 3rd Armored Division, in the van of US VII Corps (First US Army) met up at Lippstadt with the US 8th Armored Division (Ninth US Army) who were advancing from Haltern. Major-General Rose, commanding the 3rd Armored Division was killed during the day. As a result of the link-up, the German Army Group B, comprising twenty-one divisions, was to all intents and purposes encircled. To reduce this so-called 'Ruhr Pocket', General Bradley, commander of 12 Army Group, now formed the separate Fifteenth US Army under Lieutenant-General Leonard T. Gerow, with five corps, including the specially formed XXII and XXIII Corps comprising eighteen divisions taken from the First and Ninth US Armies.

The Germans started to evacuate parts of Holland still occupied by them. The First French Army advanced a further twelve miles after crossing the Rhine. Sopron, south-east of Vienna, was taken by the Russians and Marshal Konev captured the fortress of Glogow on the Oder. An Allied War Crimes Commission placed Hitler's name at the head of their list.

**Monday 2 April** Second British Army forces captured jet fighter bases at Rheine and Munster.

**Tuesday 3 April** In the east, Marshal Tolbukhin captured Wiener Neustadt.

**Wednesday 4 April** US and French forces reached Kassel, Gotha, Karlsruhe and Aschaffenburg. Hungary was by now cleared of German forces by the Russians who were now driving towards Vienna; Marshal Malinovsky captured Bratislava.

**Thursday 5 April** British forces captured Minden. Osnabruk was taken and

*Winston Churchill climbing aboard a Buffalo in preparation for his personal crossing of the Rhine*

the River Weser crossed. The Seventh US Army captured Würzburg in the valley of the Main, and eighteen US divisions began to tighten the ring round the 'Ruhr Pocket'. At this late stage of the war the Russians decided to repudiate the Soviet-Japan neutrality pact that had been signed in April 1941.

**Friday 6 April** British XII Corps, commanded by Lieutenant-General Ritchie, crossed the River Aller, a tributary of the Weser. Canadian II Corps, under Lieutenant-General Simonds, liberated the Dutch towns of Zutphen and Almelo. The Americans entered Hamm, an important railway centre that had received attention from Allied bombers throughout the war. In the east, the Russians entered the suburbs of Vienna, and launched a final assault on the town of Königsberg.

**Saturday 7 April** General Patton's Third US Army discovered a huge hoard of Nazi gold hidden in a salt mine near Merkers. French paratroops dropped in Holland north of the Zuider Zee in the area of Assem and Meppel. Allied bombers were still active: RAF Mosquitoes raided Berlin for the first time from Continental bases and 8th USAAF planes made a series of attacks on German airfields and railways.

**Sunday 8 April** Seventh US Army entered Schweinfurt. First French Army captured Pforzheim. RAF bombers sank six U-Boats in a raid on Hamburg. Colonel-General Schörner was promoted to be the last Wehrmacht Field Marshal in the Second World War.

**Monday 9 April** Seventh US Army occupied the Krupps works on the outskirts of Essen. Königsberg was finally taken by the Russians after a fifty-nine day siege; Marshal Tolbukhin's troops forced their way into the centre of Vienna. RAF bombers sank the battleship *Admiral Scheer* at Kiel and left the *Admiral Hipper* badly damaged. 8th USAAF bombers attacked jet fighters at their bases at Munich and Berlin areas. On 9 and 10 April, 357 German fighters were destroyed on the ground.

**Tuesday 10 April** Hanover captured by Ninth US Army. The First French Army took the town of Herrenalbon in the Black Forest. A final Luftwaffe sortie was made over Britain by an Ar 234 jet reconnaissance aircraft.

**Wednesday 11 April** Ninth US Army reached the River Elbe at Barby near Magdeburg; the 83rd Division then being only 75 miles from Berlin. Other American successes of the day were the capture of Brunswick and Essen. The Third US Army captured an underground V2 rocket factory at Nordhausen. Canadian II Corps crossed the River Ijssel. In Vienna the Russians crossed the Danube Canal. Spain broke off diplomatic relations with Japan.

**Thursday 12 April** The US 83rd Division crossed the Elbe near Magdeburg. Third US Army captured Weimar. In the clearance of the 'Ruhr Pocket', General Gerow's Fifteenth US Army now occupied the entire Ruhr coal basin.

Franklin D. Roosevelt died at age of 63, Harry S. Truman being immediately sworn in as President of the USA.

**Friday 13 April** Third US Army captured Jena, Naumburg and Saalfeld. Ninth US Army reached Wolmirstadt on the Elbe after covering 85 miles in three days. Vienna was now under the control of Marshal Tolbukhin's forces. Chile declared war on Japan.

**Saturday 14 April** Canadian II Corps completed the occupation of Leeuwarden area. Canadians also captured Arnhem after fierce resistance, the bridge being destroyed before the Germans retreated. Halle taken by VII Corps of First US Army also captured Bayreuth. The 'Ruhr Pocket' was cut in two from north to south by Fifteenth US Army. Colonel-General Harpe of Fifth Panzer Army ordered Army Group B to cease fighting in the absence of the commander Field Marshal Model, who could not be found. In the Atlantic, Operation TEARDROP was organised to carry out an urgent search for *Seawolf* U-Boat group thought to be carrying V2 rockets to be launched against New York.

**Sunday 15 April** Colditz castle prisoner-of-war camp liberated. The Canadians reached the sea in Northern Holland. First US Army captured Leuna. The 2nd Armored Division of the Ninth US Army was forced to withdraw from its bridgehead over the Elbe after a pontoon bridge was destroyed by enemy action. There was still fighting in France; code-named Operation VENERABLE, French and US troops attacked the 'Royan Pocket' (Gironde). The 8th USAAF struck with napalm bombs and the battle-ship *Lorraine* supported with bombardment. All German resistance in the 'Royan Pocket' ceased on 20 April.

*The final stages of the building of the first Bailey pontoon bridge across the Rhine*

**Monday 16 April** Canadian II Corps liberated Gröningen in Northern Holland. Nuremberg was reached by the Seventh US Army. Marshal Zhukov opened the Russian offensive on Berlin. RAF Lancasters raided Swinemunde and crippled the *Lützow*. In the Baltic, 6,220 refugees were drowned when the German transport ship *Goya* was sunk by Soviet submarine L3.

**Tuesday 17 April** RAF Mosquitoes bombed the Gestapo headquarters at Odense, Denmark.

**Wednesday 18 April** British Royal Engineers began building a semi-permanent Bailey bridge over the Rhine near Rees. The Canadian I Corps reached the Zuider Zee in Holland. General Patton's US V Corps crossed the Czech border. The 'Ruhr Pocket' was at last neutralised when German Army Group B surrendered; 317,000 prisoners were taken, including twenty-nine generals. Field Marshal Model had committed suicide but this was not to be known for four months. The RAF dropped 5,000 tons of bombs on Heligoland. Oberst Steinhof – a German air ace with 175 victories – suffered horrific burns when he crashed in a Me 262 jet near Munich. Steinhof recovered and became Commander-in-Chief of the post-war Luftwaffe.

**Thursday 19 April** British VIII Corps, commanded by Lieutenant-General Sir Evelyn H. Barker, reached the Elbe opposite Lauenburg. General Patch's Seventh US Army broke through the walls of Nuremberg to eliminate a fanatical SS garrison. The First US Army captured Leipzig. The Russians secured a bridgehead over the River Neisse and pushed on towards Dresden.

**Friday 20 April** The 'Stars and Stripes' was raised by the Seventh US Army over the rostrum of Nuremberg stadium, the scene of many Nazi rallies. General de Tassigny's First French Army quickly advanced along the Neckar Valley to trap German forces in the Black Forest; the 5th Armoured Division surrounded Tübingen which surrendered after two days, when 28,000 prisoners were taken. The Russians reached the suburbs of Berlin.

**Saturday 21 April** Patton's US XX Corps reached Saxony and the vicinity of Chemitz; VIII Corps was beyond Plauen, and VII Corps changed direction from east to south-east and was in Bavaria, well beyond Bayreuth. The First French Army occupied Stuttgart. The Russian Marshal Koniev attacked north of Dresden. The USSR and the 'Lublin' government in Poland signed a twenty-year mutual assistance pact.

**Sunday 22 April** Third US Army in drive towards Regensberg. Seventh US Army captured a bridge over the River Dillingen. The Russians began a pincer attack on Berlin and captured the Weissensee district. Hitler decided to stay in Berlin. Himmler met Count Bernadotte of the Swedish Red Cross in an attempt to initiate armistice negotiations with Britain and the USA; this overture was rejected by the Allies on 27 April.

**Monday 23 April** Marshal Zhukov's troops captured Frankfort an der Oder. RAF Coastal Command bombers hit five German merchant ships. Blackout regulations lifted in Britain.

**Tuesday 24 April** Dachau concentration camp liberated. British XXX Corps reached Bremen suburbs in face of fierce opposition from 2nd Kriegsmarine. The troops of Marshal Koniev and Zhukov link up in the suburbs of Berlin. The British Treasury disclose that the war has cost £274,000 million up to 31 March 1945.

**Wednesday 25 April** First US Army patrols made contact with Russians near Torgau on the River Elbe. The Seventh US Army crossed the Danube on an 80 mile front capturing German XIII Korps and its commander, Lieutenant-General Count d'Oriola. Marshals Koniev and Zhukov completed ring round Berlin at Potsdam. The RAF bomb Berchtesgaden (Hitler's Eagles Nest) and German coastal batteries at Wangerooge in the Frisian Islands. The 8th USAAF bombed the Skoda works at Pilsen, Czechoslovakia. At the San Francisco Conference the text of the United Nations Charter was begun; it was completed by 23 June and signed on 26 June.

**Thursday 26 April** The Guards Armoured division occupied Cuxhaven at the mouth of the River Elbe. Second British Army captured Bremen. Stettin captured. Third US Army took Brno in Czechoslovakia; Patton also crossed the Danube in the Regensburg sector. General Hodges of the First US Army met Colonel-General Zhadov, commander of the Soviet Fifth Guards Army, at Torgau. Russians captured the Dahlem and Siemensstadt districts of Berlin. Göring dismissed for proposing separate peace with the Western Powers; Von Greim appointed Commander-in Chief of the Luftwaffe in Göring's place.

*A pontoon bridge is opened over the Rhine*

**Friday 27 April** Regensberg captured by Third US Army. Russians in possession of Potsdam, Spandau and Rathenow suburbs of Berlin as well as the central district of Neuköln and Templehof. Horrific descriptions of Buchenwald concentration camp published in Britain. Marshal Pétain surrendered to French officials arriving from Switzerland.

**Saturday 28 April** Allies crossed the River Elbe. Troops of Seventh US Army liberated family of Colonel Count Klaus von Stauffenberg (who attempted the assassination of Hitler) at Niederdorf in the South Tyrol. Major Braum and two hundred German troops attempted a coup in Munich; they seized the radio station and tried to kidnap Gauleiter Geisler but the uprising was put down by SS bodyguards. Mussolini, the Italian ex-Dictator, and his mistress, Clara Petacci, executed by Italian partisans at Dongo on Lake Como. The bodies were publicly exhibited in a Milan square.

**Sunday 29 April** The Second British Army captured Lauenburg, trapping German forces in Denmark. Russians captured Moabit power station and Anhalter railway terminus in Berlin. German Army representatives in Italy signed unconditional surrender at Caserta: one million troops were ordered to cease fire on 2 May. Hitler nominated Grand Admiral Karl Doenitz as his successor, married Eva Braun, and dictated his 'Political Testament'. At sea there was the last battle between a U-Boat pack and Allied convoy escorts; two U-Boats were destroyed but U 427 survived the blast from 678 depth charges; the frigate *Goodall* was sunk.

**Monday 30 April** Russians reached the Reichstag building in Berlin. Adolf Hitler committed suicide in the Führerbunker in Berlin at 15.30 hours.

**Tuesday 1 May** Lieutenant-General Wolz offered the surrender of Hamburg to Second British Army. Russians captured Charlottenburg and Schoeneburg districts of Berlin. Goebbels and his wife poisoned their six children and then committed suicide.

**Wednesday 2 May** British 6th Airborne Division met the 70th Russian Armoured Division (Marshal Rokossovsky's lead formation) at Wismer on the Baltic. British 11th Armoured Division, commanded by Major-General Roberts, captured Lübeck for VIII Corps. Patton's 13th Armored Division, under Major-General Millikin, crossed the River Inn at Braunau (Hitler's birthplace). Dr Wernher von Braun, General Dornberger and other rocket experts surrendered to the US 44th Division of the Seventh US Army near Reutte in Austrian Tyrol. Munich occupied by US XV Corps. Josef Stalin announced the fall of Berlin in an Order of the Day: 'Troops of the 1st Byelorussian Front, commanded by Marshal Zhukov have today May 2 completely captured Berlin hotbed of German aggression.' The Russians also captured the ports of Rostock and Warnemunde. The last RAF raid on Europe was by Mosquitoes on Kiel, while at sea the RAF sank 23 out of 60 U-Boats attempting to escape from Germany to Norway.

**Thursday 3 May** The surrender of Hamburg to British forces was completed; fifty-nine German merchant ships and six hundred small craft were scuttled in the port. The III Corps of Patton's Third US Army captured Braunau, Hitler's birthplace. Field Marshal Montgomery received German envoy at his Tactical Headquarters on Lüneburg Heath. Tragically, some 5,000 former concentration camp prisoners were drowned when RAF bombers sank the liner *Cap Arkona* and ss *Thielbek* off Lübeck. Queen Wilhelmina and Princess Juliana returned to the Netherlands from exile. The Prime Minister of Eire, Eamonn De Valéra, offered condolences to the German Legation on the death of Hitler; and the Portuguese dictator, Antonio de Oliveira Salazar, called for a day of mourning.

**Friday 4 May** The first of a series of German surrenders took place at Field Marshal Montgomery's Tactical Headquarters on Lüneberg Heath, where Admiral von Friedburg and other representatives of the German High Command signed an armistice surrendering all German forces in North-West Germany, Denmark, Holland and Dunkirk (the latter had been a pocket of resistance throughout the campaign since it had been by-passed in the advance from Normandy).

The Allied advance in Germany continued, notwithstanding the surrender; the British 7th Armoured Division, commanded by Major-General Lyne, captured intact a bridge over the Kiel Canal at Eckernförde. The US 3rd Division crossed the Brenner Pass and met the 88th Division of the US 5th Army at Vipiteno. The French 2nd Division occupied Berghof and just missed Hermann Göring; in five weeks campaigning the French 1st Army had destroyed eight German divisions and taken 180,000 prisoners, including the son of Field Marshal Erwin Rommel.

**Saturday 5 May** General Schutz, the last commander of German Army Group B, surrendered at General Jacob L. Dever's Headquarters of 6 Army

*The Prime Minister and Lieutenant-General Sir Miles C. Dempsey visiting units by jeep on 26 March*

Group. General Maczek's 1st Polish Armoured Division (at the time attached to the Second Canadian Army) had advanced within nine miles of Wilhelmshaven, and the 5th Canadian Armoured Division was on the outskirts of Emden. The last U-Boat action off the American coast took place: U 853 sank the *ss Black Prince* and in turn was sunk by *USS Atherton*.

**Sunday 6 May** The Third US Army met the 3rd Ukranian Front troops coming up the Danube at Linz; Patton's forces also occupied the Skoda works but Eisenhower ordered the Third Army not to advance further into Czechoslovakia. In the meantime, three German SS Divisions were ordered to crush an uprising in Prague. Portugal deemed it prudent to break off diplomatic relations with Germany.

**Monday 7 May** This was the day of the second of three German surrenders, this one at General Eisenhower's SHAEF Headquarters at Rheims, France, in the presence of representatives of the United States, Great Britain, the Soviet Union and France. Colonel-General Alfred Jodl, Chief-of-Staff OKW, and Admiral Hans von Friedburg, acting for Grand Admiral Karl Doenitz, signed an instrument which provided for the unconditional surrender of all German forces on all fronts.

Allied troops occupied Emden and Wilhelmshaven, and moved into East Holland and Denmark. The Hungarian Prime Minister, Szalasi, was captured by the Seventh US Army near Salzburg, and the Hungarian crown jewels were found in a railway carriage. The siege of Breslau ended after 60 days with 40,000 Germans surrendering to the Russians. At sea, the day saw the war's final U-Boat actions: U 2336 sank the coasters *Avondale Park* and *Sneland* off the Firth of Forth, and the last U-Boat to be destroyed by the

55

*D Day Plus Two (26 March). The gliders are by now an accepted part of the scenery as a self-propelled gun passes a landing zone*

Allies at sea, U 320, was sunk by a RAF Catalina flying-boat off Bergen.

Spain, neutral throughout the war, but with strong sympathies with the Axis powers, now broke off diplomatic relations with Germany.

**Tuesday 8 May** British Prime Minister Winston Churchill and the President of the United States Harry S. Truman declared the war with Germany ended at one minute past midnight and that this would be VE (Victory in Europe) Day.

Dresden was occupied by the Russians. The German garrison in Prague surrendered. Crown Prince Olav returned to Norway and proclaimed the surrender of all German occupation forces. The Channel Islands were liberated.

In Berlin the final act of surrender was signed at sixteen minutes past midnight in a building formerly housing the Pioneer College of the Wehrmacht in the suburb of Karlshorst. The German delegates were General Field Marshal Wilhelm Keitel, Chief of the Wehrmacht Supreme Command; Admiral Hans von Friedburg, Commander-in-Chief of the Kriegsmarine, and General Stumpf, of the Luftwaffe.

At midnight the German commanders were ushered into a room draped with British, American, Russian and French national flags. In the presence of Marshal Zhukov, Field Marshal Keitel was asked by Air Chief Marshal Sir Arthur Tedder whether he understood the terms of unconditional surrender. On replying in the affirmative, he, Admiral von Friedburg and General Stumpf signed for Germany, the Allied signatories being Marshal Zhukov for the Soviet Union High Command, and Air Chief Marshal Tedder for the Allied Expeditionary Force. Lieutenant-General Carl A.

Spaatz, Commander of the US Strategic Air Forces, and General de Lattre de Tassigny, Commander of the First French Army, also signed as witnesses.

The final days of war in Europe were over at last.

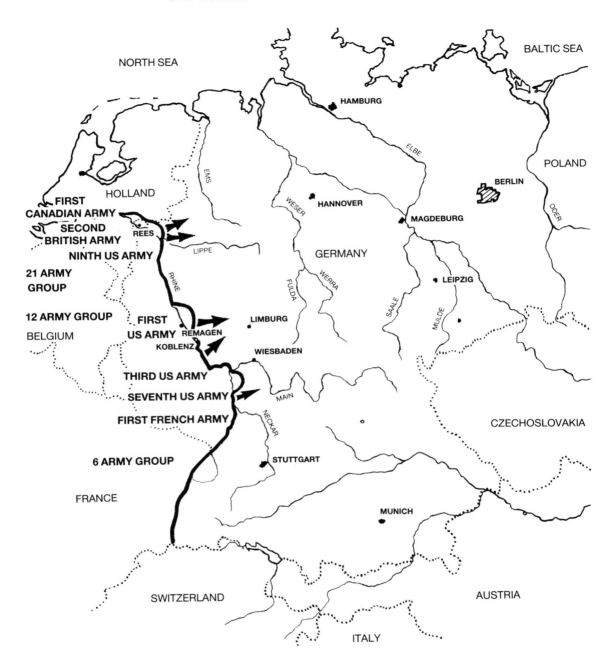

**Map 1:  Western Front 27 March 1945**

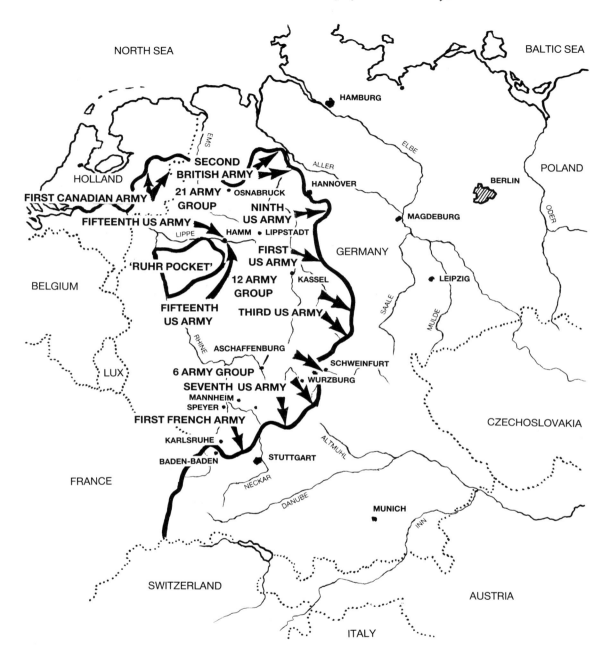

**Map 2:  Western Front 9 April 1945**

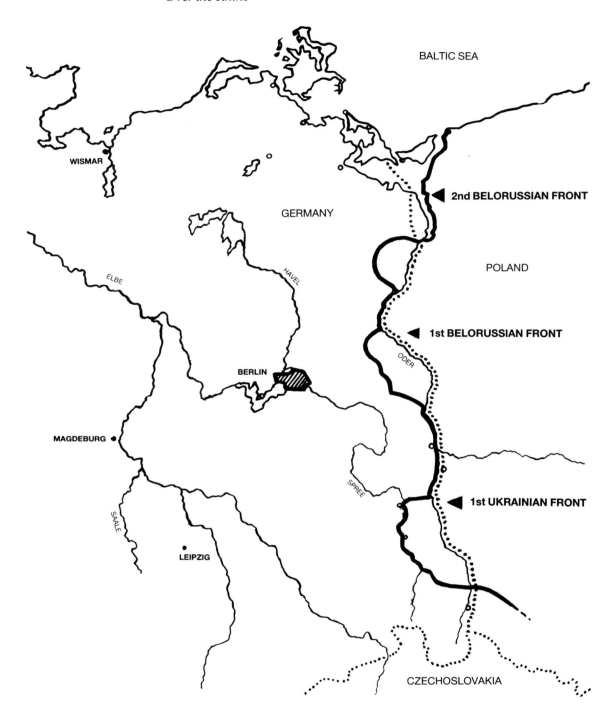

**Map 3: Eastern Front 18 April 1945**

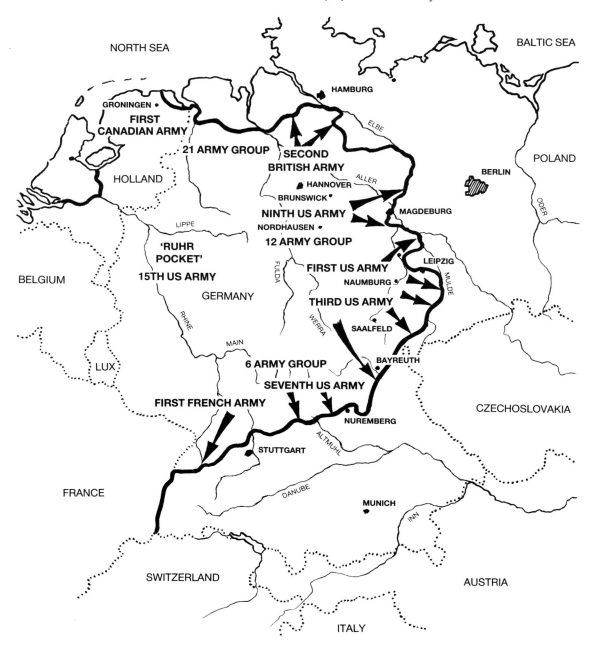

**Map 4: Western Front 19 April 1945**

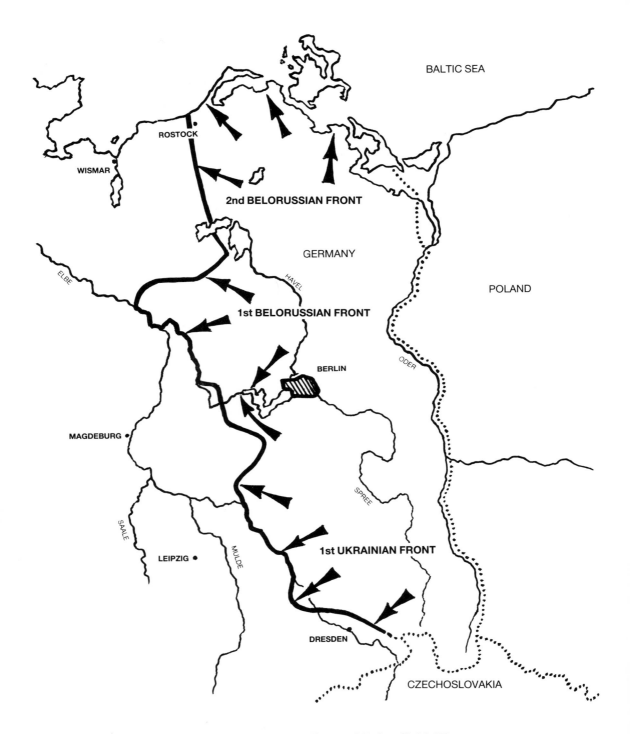

**Map 5: Eastern Front 25 April 1945**

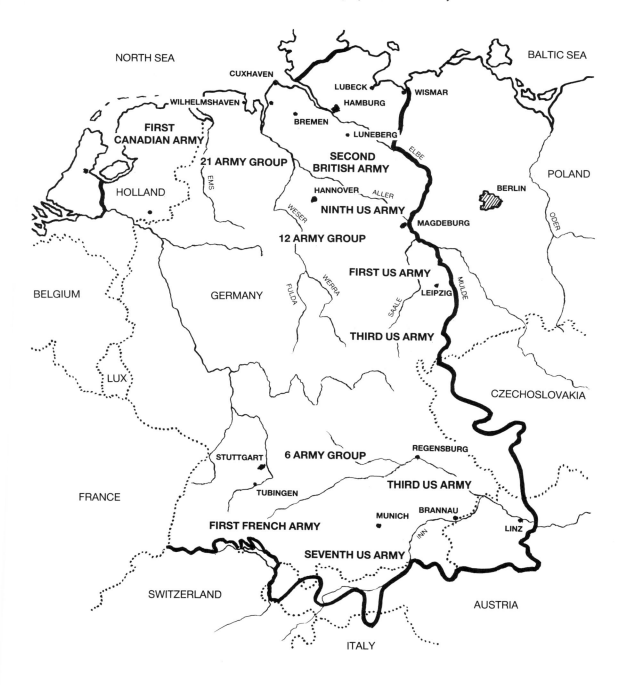

**Map 6:  Western Front 7 May 1945**

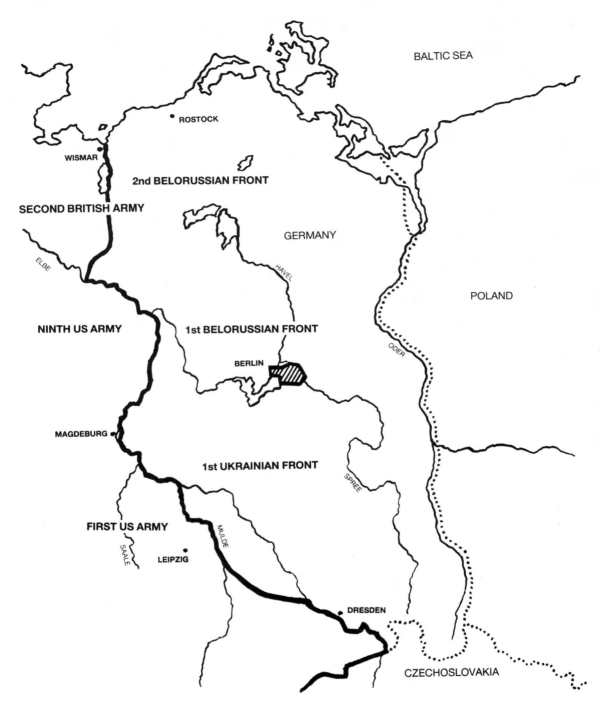

**Map 7: Eastern and Western Fronts Meet
Position at 8 May 1945**